LACONICS OF CULT

LACONICS OF CULT

by
INGERSOLL LOCKWOOD

edited by
KASEY JAMES ELLIOTT

Independent Publishing 2018

COPYRIGHT

Independently published 2018

Printed in the United States of America

First published by Private Printing 1910

Cover designed by the editor

ISBN: 9781792950414

"The gods that exist are born of those that exist no longer." — *Rigveda*

"The idea which man calls 'god' only exists in the consciousness of man himself." — *Edward Bulwer-Lytton*

"We do not resemble him, he resembles us." — *Ibid*

INGERSOLL LOCKWOOD

LAWYER AND AUTHOR

(At the age of 35)

INGERSOLL LOCKWOOD

AUTHOR AND ORIGINATOR OF THE CULT OF THE IMMORTAL HUMAN

(At the age of 60)

PREFACE

There is but one form of human enslavement more villainous and more detestable than the chains of the tyrant or the shackles of the despot, and that is the enslavement of the human mind under ecclesiastical tyranny, whose cowering and crouching victims at the crack of the priestly lash are driven from the cultivation of their own intelligence, from the custody of their own thoughts, from the guardianship of their own souls, and who, like whipped dogs, trembling and whining in abject submission at the feet of the oppressor, lick the very hand that wields the lash. I'm well aware what a thankless task it is to attack the established order of things, theological, political or ethical, for in my long life I have often heard the old cry in different forms: Great is Diana of the Ephesians! But I make no excuse or apology for my little book.

If it shall turn a single man or woman away from the old path of Superstition, for so many centuries beaten hard and smooth by the tread of millions of poor tired human feet pressing forward in the dust of out-worn ecclesiastical "props" that line the way in search of something they never can find, I will be satisfied.

I owe this dear country something for my enjoyment of all these years of the priceless privilege of liberty and the pursuit of happiness, and this be my gift to my countrymen, for I set no copyright upon it; it belongs to anybody who can use it, and if the clerics, theologs, priests, *et id omne genus,* can't bless it — which I should hardly expect, let them use it as a remedy for torpid liver and heartily cure it.

I have only one favor to ask of any man or woman who may pick it up, and that is this: Read it through before you pass judgement upon it.

I'm entitled to that much consideration anyway. If monarchs only had the time to read the petitions tremblingly handed up to them, there would be more justice done in the world.

Ingersoll Lockwood
Saratoga Springs, New York
May 1, 1910

SUPERSTITION

I have often pictured myself as the last priest of imperial Rome, standing in an attitude of superb dignity by the side if his alter and saying to his Christian successor, who had entered the Roman temple with some fear and trembling — even though a squad of converted soldiers was at his heels, to take possession of the premises: *Moriturus, te saluto!* And then adding with a long and deep-drawn sigh: And yet, Christian brother, it will be but a change in form and not in substance, for all religions are the same, being the offspring of man's brain, they cannot differ greatly. The people must have their *lares* and *penates* in their homes and their statues and images in the temples. They must have at the hand of the priest their signs, wonders, and miracles just as they look for their *panem et circenses* at the hands of the political leaders: or else you will lose control. How was it possible to make a more sublime god than our Father Jove, god of gods. *Zeu kudiste, megiste, kelainephes, aitheri naion!* (Thou Jove, most honored, greatest of all, wrapped in thy dark majesty. Dweller in infinite space!). Can't you improve upon our cloud-encircled heaven, set high above the reach of man, with its wondrous glory of light and color, echoing to the deafening crash of Jove's thunderbolts or lighted up by the blinding flash of his lightning as he robs some blasphemer of his sight forever? It has often been tried, but the world comes ever back to us for our recipe.

Be kind to the beloved messengers of our gods, Olympian servitors, the dainty Iris, the exquisite Psyche, the sweet boy Eros, the winged Mercury, guide and comfort of departed souls, you will need them all, for even gods must be served. Turn not from our sacred Vestal Virgins, keepers of the altar fires. They are greatly beloved of the people. Even the rude soldiers bend and kiss their shadows as they pass.

"We do! We do!" muttered warriors of the squad and then suddenly remembering their new faith, a deep scarlet shone through the dark visages tanned by Afric's sun. "Brother," continued the priest, "you will need a Queen of Heaven. I cannot too highly recommend our superb Juno, guardian of the marriage tie. It is to her we owe our matchless Roman mothers.

I know little of your Jewish demi-god. We do not love the Jews in imperial capital. They are the butt of our ridicule on the stage, soaked in credulity and Superstition. Our great poet Horace says: *Credat Judaeus Apella!* But I have read in the *Acta Diurna* that your new god's birthday falls in the latter part of December. Our *Saturnalia,* a favorite festival with our people, falls upon the 16th, 17th, and 18th of that month, so it would be the simplest thing in the world to unite the two. The people must have their religious pomps and parades. Our slaves, too, will not be satisfied without this brief relaxation of their servitude.

And finally, brother, I commend to thy adoption these beautiful altars and priestly vestments. Noble show! Stately ministrations of which our Imperial Master the Emperor, our Supreme Pontiff, is so justly proud. It was impossible to increase its beauty and magnificence. Take, brother, what the world summons us to surrender and farewell. Once again I cry: *Moriturus, te salute!"*

As he turned from the altar, a great crowd of acolytes, augurs, choristers, thurifers, train-bearers, and the like swarmed out and fell upon their knees. The stately priest moved away, with his head of Apollo high in the air, his right hand uplifted, with thumb, first, and second fingers extended, his superb seal ring bearing a Jove's head upon it glistening in the dim light. The crowd of ministrants followed him forth in dead silence.

When they had disappeared, the Christian priest made a sign to the soldiers to fall back, and taking out from under his gown a small silver vessel containing water and an aspersorium, he sprinkled the top and sides of the altar while muttering prayers, and then with much hand-waving, which the soldiers watched half shamefacedly, he sank upon his knees, the blood stains of the last sacrifice scarcely dry upon the white marble floor beneath his.

$$*\qquad*\qquad*\qquad*\qquad*\qquad*$$

Recipe to make a god:

Take 33 1/3% Ignorance, 33 1/3% Credulity, and 33 1/3% Human Ingenuity. Mix carefully, and let stand until fermentation sets in. Then add *quant. suf.* extract of the Miraculous, and vary the strength of the mixture to suit powers of resistance of locality.

This is the time and it may be justly termed a specific. When Jove was first set up in business as a *deus deorum,* that is, as the absorber of many smaller gods, he proved to be altogether too harsh a remedy for the people to whom it was administered. Prometheus undertook the task of reforming him. It was a severe struggle, but Prometheus succeeded admirably and eventually made Jove one of the grandest, noblest, and honest gods that the world has ever seen. The same thing happened with Jahveh, the Jewish god. Before the Christians could accept him, he had to be completely made over, severely disciplined, stripped of many of his old habits, and put under bonds as to his future behavior. Then he was rechristened Jehovah.

Allah likewise, as first designed by Mahomet was not at all acceptable to the Arabians. The god-maker was given very plainly to understand that radical changes must be made in the character, attributes, and pretensions of Allah in order to make him acceptable to the people. This was done, and today a hundred million human beings answer to his call for prayers.

*   *   *   *   *   *

As the stream cannot rise higher than its source, it follows very naturally that no god can outlive the civilization that creates him. There is an exception to this general rule and that is in the case of an old god made over, "modernized" in fact, for the use of a succeeding civilization. This accounts for Jahveh's long reign when other old gods have gone into eternal night, gods who once contemporary with him, and even more powerful and active than he was. For instance, we may ask: Where are the gods of old, the gods of mighty Egypt,

Osiris, Apis, Orus, and their crew,

under whose reign the arts and sciences achieved such results as even now to astound the world? Where is ibis-headed Thoth, jackal-headed Anubis, the "lackey" of the gods of his day as Mercury was of his? Where are these old, old gods, from whom Moses pilfered his knowledge of mystical lore? All dissolved into finer and more impalpable dust than kings, commons, and slaves who worshipped you.

You gods, you gods, whether you sit on great white thrones resting on no more substantial foundation than a summer cloud, or whether you reign in the Tartarean vaults of dusky Hades, you must one day, one day, go down to your twilight and to your eternal night!

And I may ask too: Where is Jove, magnificent Jove, that "divine gentleman" under whose superb reign the world attained to its dizziest heights of art, literature, philosophy, and mathematics? You glorious masterpiece of human ingenuity, you "awful Jove, whom young Phidias brought from no vain or shallow thought," whose head remains today the very mold and pattern of all really great gods, benignant, just, and sensible enough not to kick against the pricks of Fate, where are you?

Faded like clouds from the sky,
To share no more in our mortal strife
Or come at a hero's cry,
They white throne stands enshrouded in gloom
And the night birds perch above
Where joyously pealed the Olympian laugh
And shimmered the smile of love.

And Jahveh, too, where are you, cruel, jealous, and bloody-minded cousin of Moloch himself, you "fine flower" of the imagination of nomadic, parasitic, imitative, unassimilable, and often enslaved net of tribes, whose mythology set beside the exquisite creations of father Jove's is but the smut on the ear, god of shreds and patches gathered up by your people in their wanderings and enslavements, your people, who when Homer's fingers were trembling on his divine lyre were only able to emit the caterwaulings of despair over their own shortcomings, your people who have left no literature, except this, no songs that the world sings, no architecture, no sculpture, you whose sacred books reek with odor of sexual disequilibrium, you whose prophets wove about thee such a tight-fitting and enveloping shirt of Nessus of Superstition, that you were kept in a state of eternal unrest and ill humor, where are you, I ask? *Hic et ubique!* Who knows? I defy any one of your prophets, any dozen of them, to locate you.

* * * * * *

Who are you, Jahveh, who has removed your Jewish gabardine and, under your new name of Jehovah, pretends to sit in judgment on this majestic world of ours? You claim to have created this great universe, illimitable, unfathomable, and immeasurable, in six days, while science assures us that for millions upon millions of years it has been slowly and gradually unfolding from simple beginnings until now, when man, immortal man, the maker of his own gods, crowns the majestic dome of nature's evolution! In that wonderful workshop of man's imagination, in which, especially during childhood of the world, gods and devils were turned out with almost startling readiness, there has always lain a foot-ruler to measure them by, to wit, their so-called "bibles." Let us apply my own foot-ruler to you and measure you up. You say that having caused a deep sleep to fall upon Adam, you took out one of his ribs, having care to close up the opening, and that from that rib you made a woman and brought her unto Adam. You were not aware that for ages before you were set up in business by Moses, nature had been making both men and women, and that upon the bodies of each she had always been accustomed to set her most unmistakable hallmark! Describe your woman that we may see whether she was so stamped or not. And you said also that you did set your bow in the cloud so that when you looked upon it you would remember a certain everlasting covenant. Ah! Why was Moses not honest enough to tell you that for millions of years before he created you, nature had herself set that beautiful bow in the cloud? Ay, and set it, too, on the earth wherever any child might cause crystal drops of water to dance in the sunshine. No more, that here, there, and everywhere where under certain conditions the crystal drops were hung like a gossamer veil in the rays of the moonlight, there nature unrolled her spectral arch of beauty.

And you said also, that you did snatch certain mortals, Enoch and Elijah, from the face of the earth without letting them see death. Unbeknown to you that other gods had done the same, that the people expected these things from them, that Father Jove often showed his power by performing such wonderful acts, as witness his taking of the beautiful boy Ganymede, and his lifting to the stars many others who had died on earth, and admitting them into the theocorp!

*   *   *   *   *   *

LACONICS OF CULT

Not a despot, tyrant, oppressor of the people, or
contemner of the rights of man claims to hold his throne by
"divine right," to be the "anointed" of some god, to be entitled
by special dispensation of heaven to set his heel upon the necks
of his fellow men. Not a driver of slaves, robber of the toil of
man or millionaire who greases the axles of his chariot wheels
with the marrow of human bones, that do not "love God," is not
as regular to prayer call as any Muslim that ever clove a dog of a
Christian with his scimitar and wiped the blade on his shirt to
wear the crimson seal as a testimony of his zeal in Allah's service,
and not with a feeling of self-blessedness make punctual payment
of his tithes to maintain the due and godly service of altar,
chancel, choir, incense, and priestly robes and the richly-walled
temple that enclose them all, for the glorification of an imaginary
being whom they have set up for selfish purposes. Do you think
that this "establishment" will ever rid men's hearts of their
distrust of each other, equalize conditions so that abject poverty
shall not gaze with hatred and defiance at the curtained windows
of the rich, with curses for those within? Never! Never! So long
as men turn not from false gods of Superstition to the real ones
of human love, human sympathy, human mutual assistance. Look
at our sister Republic of France! The "establishment" has existed
within her limits from the second century of the Common Era.
In the due course of time, it spread to every nook and corner of
the land, permeated every stratum of life from the highest to the
lowest, no crack or crevice could escape it. It stood in the hovel,

11

in the home, in the castle, in the palace. Man opened and closed his eyes on the crucifix. Childhood's tiny hands told off its beads. Cowled monks and dark-garbed nuns and sisters were here, there, and everywhere. The priest made choice of school books; no morsel entered human mouths without the sign of the cross. The trembling wretch listened to his sentence of death often for unsubstantiated accusation, beneath the shadow of the bleeding Prince of Peace nailed to his beam. Kings and princes trembled at the anathema of Rome. From cradle to grave, the priest, the eternal priest was in power, the guardian of thoughts and consciences. He knew all, saw all, excused, approved, or condemned all. And what was the result of this reign of god? Or, had I not better say, of this mad and unrestrained riot of Superstition? Every other human being living and breathing in that god-favored land today was born out of wedlock. But at last an awakening has come. Superstition has been toppled from its gilded niche and human reason has every chance of coming to its own again.

*   *   *   *   *   *

In the name of common sense, why did man ever set up these shadowy tyrants to tease, worry, and torment him? The answer is a very simple one: If you chain even an intelligent dog in the moonlight, he will lay at it; if you shut a child in a dark room he will tremble and send forth a cry of terror; if you place a savage in a position to look upon any great convulsion of nature's forces, he will shiver and cower in abject fear — dog, child, and savage, all three stand upon the same plane of evolution. The dog runs to his master, the child to its parent, the savage to its idol of baked mud — for protection, the dog with its caress, the child with its kiss of thankfulness, the savage with his gift of food to appease the evil spirit.

In other words, the first god that man set up was an attempt to appease the wrath of nature. The progression was easy. In a higher grade of mental development when the primitive man moved his habitation hither and thither he came into contact with more varied forms of nature's apparent unfriendliness to him. The earth quaked beneath his feet, the avalanche slipped with a thunderous roar down the mountain side, the skies emptied their stores of hailstones upon his head, the thunderbolt split the towering monarch of the forest, the rivers overflowed and swept his frail habitation away, the earth sprouted boiling water, the volcano spat fire, and the wind blast whipt the ocean into the white foam of an all-threatening rage. The "medicine man" was not slow to take advantage of the situation. He encouraged the sacrifice of food to the idol of baked mud, for man is quick to shift the burden of toil upon his fellow man, and later when the meat sacrifice came into vogue, the "medicine man" found his larder well stored, for surely no one should feed upon the consecrated food, except himself. In our day of more refined Superstition, the consecrated wine that is left over must be drunk by the ministrant. Now you are in a position to understand why the odor of the roasting flesh of the lamb and kid was so pleasing to Jahveh, and why Goethe makes Mephisto assure Faust that the church has the power to digest any kind of offering. And mark well that, while primitive man's abject fear in the presence of nature's convulsions was perfectly natural, yet the subtle and ever increasing encouragement of his Superstition by the "medicine man" and his "successors and assigns" was the first act of human tyranny that was destined to take on such vast strength and colossal proportions as to crowd the crowned and sceptered despot quite out of business. And now, even in this free land of ours, where liberty sits enthroned in superb majesty and the rights of man are given in large letters on brazen tablets, the rabbi, prelate, clergyman, priest, parson, and their thousands of assistants, curates, deacons, acolytes, clerics, elders, and presbyters stand ready upon the slightest attempt to loosen their hold upon the people, to raise the old cry in different words: Great is Diana of the Ephesians! Great is Diana of the Ephesians!

*   *   *   *   *   *

But after all, Jahveh is but a machine god to be wheeled out as occasion may demand, and 999 times out of a thousand to cover with his name and majesty and with the additional prestige of some members of the theocorp — such as Hamlet called upon: "Angels and ministers of grace!" — some act of human meanness, some bit of hypocrisy, some impending intent to do as unethical act; e.g. to curse an enemy — in which case one commonly sees not only Jahveh himself but the leading members of the theocrop dragged out *ad hoc*; to cover up a perjury about to be committed, or some wrongful act against a fellow man for whom the jurant's affection or friendship has cooled, or against one whom he is about to deceive for some selfish purpose, in which case he calls loudly upon Jahveh to *teste* as the lawyers say the righteousness of his intentions.

Or, it may be that the drawing of Jahveh's name into play is for the purpose of sanctifying some very act forbidden by the god himself, such as war, pillage, robbing, or wronging a weaker foe.

Or, in the mouths of the priests to curse the unbeliever, non-conformer, or person indifferent to his circumstantial and ornate anathema, or to the sanctity of his excommunication by book, bell, and candle.

The old German emperor during the Franco-German war never failed to thank god upon any special occasion when a particularly large number of Frenchmen were slain in battle by the long range Krupp guns which had been perfected by this god-fearing nation for the very purpose of getting even with the *rothe Hosen* for the Napoleonic invasion of the fatherland. Now to be perfectly logical, when the priests, as they do in their almost daily commendation of their god as "omnipotent," pledge him (of course for value received) as safe and sure to be depended upon in any emergency, why should not the poor Frenchmen have treated their god in the same as the African savages do theirs when he leaves them in the lurch in a pitched battle against a neighboring tribe, to wit: tie ropes around the necks of their idols and drag them through the filth and mud and mire to punish them for not doing their duty and living up to representations made by the medicine men? It could be that the priests sometime in the near future will be forced to say of the proclaimed attribute of omnipotency as the proprietors of storage warehouses do of the words "absolutely fireproof," that they are not to be taken as a guarantee but as being "merely descriptive."

*   *   *   *   *   *

Alas, poor mortals, how you cudgeled your brains in your attempts to make your gods worthy of the name. Homer, in the Iliad, makes the wounded Mars roar like ten thousand ordinary men, so that both Greeks and Trojans flee in nameless terror. When a wounded god falls he covers several lots of land. Even Minerva is built upon such a generous scale that when she puts on Pluto's helmet, her head is large enough to fill the vast casque. Homer lets his gods be wounded, but it is impossible to kill them, their veins being filled with ichor and not blood. The Jews, too, were always possessed of the idea that a god must be of gigantic build. So we find that when Moses hid in the cleft in the rock and Jahveh walked by, he covered Moses with one hand, so that would make him about thirty-six feet tall. The statue of the Olympian Jove by Phidias, one of the wonders of the world, was thirty-five feet in height from its base. This seems so have been about the standard height of gods. As a god Jahveh was very careful never to let Moses see his face. In the burning bush he only showed his back, and, as he walked away from the cleft in the rock, Moses was directed to be satisfied with a rear view. When the Greek gods mingled with mortals, they were often recognizable by the wonderful luminosity of their eyes. Telemachus, in his interview with Minerva, suspected at once that the stranger was a god, but he could not tell which one it was. Virgil had a notion that you could tell a goddess by her walk.

To give an idea of sublimity to Jahveh the Jews are accustomed to make use of expressions well calculated to impress the superstitious minds of the people, such as: He makes the clouds his chariot; he walks on the wings of the wind; his thunderous voice causes the waters to flow up the mountain sides; he looks upon the earth and it trembles; he touches the hills and they smolder, and so on *ad lib*.

Father Jove wraps the gigantic *manes* of Hercules in a cloud and bears him away from earth in a four horse chariot.

Jahveh, in translating Elijah, made use of a chariot of fire and horses of fire, and wafted them up to heaven by means of a whirlwind. Jove sent his eagle after the beautiful boy Ganymede, which snatched him away from the very midst of his playfellows on Mount Ida.

Deification or lifting to the stars, as practiced by Father Jove, had in view either reward of those mortals who had suffered through the purity and constancy of their affections, such as Psyche, or Callisto, and her son, whom father Jove snatched away and placed in the starry firmament as the Great and Little Bear; but more particularly those he lifted to the stars were the great benefactors of the human race, such as Astraea, the pure and lovely daughter of Themis, goddess of justice and law, counsellor of Jove himself. Astraea, goddess of innocence and purity, was removed from the wicked world and placed by Jove among the stars as Virgo, The Virgin. Cadmus the inventor of letters and Hercules the slayer of monsters that oppress man were also lifted to the stars. This system of the deification of mortals as practiced by Jahveh, the reformed and etherealized Jahveh, under and by the direction of his priests, has been and is the mere encourager of Superstition. Services to mankind are not the moving cause, but the greater or lesser muscular callosity resulting from long-continued prayer. One of these instances is that Simon Stylites of the 5th century, who remained alive for twenty-six years on the top of a column exposed naked to the elements. To describe the horrid depth of Superstition to which his worshippers sank in their baleful ignorance would defile any decent page. A lover of his kind can only emit a groan of despair. Nor has the hand of the new world been listless or idle in the art of theotecture. During the Toltec and Aztec civilization of Mexico, a very extensive and intricate theocorp, under the guidance and management of an army of priests, was in existence at the time of the arrival of that monster of cruelty Cortez, who in fact at first taken to be the Toltec messiah; no doubt from his white skin, for his smoking and flaming hell of a heart was not visible. The god Taotl was at the head of this theocorp, with thirteen assistant gods and two hundred inferior deities, under the command of their frightful Mars, Huitzilopochtli, compared to whom the Greek god was a calf-eyed infant to tenderness. Even highly civilized peoples prefer their gods terrible in threat and execution. But some will exclaim — for, with a strange incongruity in his nature, man, through a liberty loving creature, yet rather than do his own thinking and bear himself the cares of state, clings to the very yoke that his oppressor lays upon his neck — Why is it that there are so few cries of *nescio deos!*

In addition to the reason above stated there are many others: The priests have so corrupted human nature that at the least show of indifference or contempt the priest balances anathema in his hand like Father Jove ready to cast a bolt, and the parson threatens eternal damnation. Then again, man's ever present distrust of woman's virtue comes in. No matter to what horrid depths of Superstition so-called religion may descend, he calmly adds: It is good for them, women need such a shoe on their wheels in the steep descents of life. And another reason is that any and all worship of so-called celestial beings forms a most admirable shield and cover for that most despicable of all human weaknesses, hypocrisy. And last, that terrible demon ignorance, who hears, suckles, and hugs to her bosom with fiendish delight that favorite child of hers, Superstition, is always a lover of the gods. I hardly need to call your attention to the fact that outside of these and any and all other reasons why god systems have been and are so tenacious of life, is that death, and that, too, in its most awful forms, until very recent years, awaited the so-called blasphemer who even privately denounced that worship of gods as mere Superstition or asserted that all such shadowy beings are but the children of men's dread of malign spirits.

But the truth is that all down through the centuries the great thinkers, philosophers, investigators, and scientists have, with never ceasing iteration and reiteration, denounced as Superstition the theory that there are any such beings as "gods" sitting up in the clouds or anywhere else, or that there ever had been any need of such "creators," that nature showed herself to be a gradual growth, sublimely regular and systematic, with never a *saltum,* from the simplest germs endowed only with movement, to the magnificent mind of man crowning this unfolding of countless millions of years.

Lord Robert Bulwer-Lytton, in the contemplation of this question of so-called celestial beings, expresses himself in these calm but eloquent phrases:

The idea which man calls "god" only exists in the consciousness of man himself. Though we should take the wings of morning and fly to the uttermost parts of the earth, yet we can find nothing there which we have not carried with us. Whether we scale the heights or sound the depths. Mount up into heaven or go down into hell, we are equally unable to travel out of our own thoughts or attain to any point of space beyond the reach of it. Space and time are not things or even the qualities of things; they are only our manner of thinking of things, the modes and conditions of our consciousness.

We are not the masterpieces of a supreme being who has formed us in his own image, but our idea of such a being we have formed in the image of ourselves. We do not resemble him; he resembles us.

*   *   *   *   *   *

It will be urged that even Voltaire died professing a belief in a god and that he erected a church at Ferney bearing the inscription: *Deo erexit Voltaire.* The answer to this is that the time had not yet come to cry *Nescio deos!* Voltaire made a bold fight against Superstition (*L'infame*), and he was satisfied with that. The Republic of France is reaping the good effects of that fight this very moment. Had he known that it was nature that put the seashells on the tops of the Alps and not the priests, as he thought, he could have died happy.

But science was too young for that. A whole century was to elapse before nature was to be allowed to cry out: Take courage, my children, it is I, I who has done it all! For millions and millions of years I have been occupied with this work! From infinitesimal beginnings, step by step, until you, man, my child with your wonderful consciousness, stand as the crown and ornament of my unfolding, have I evolved the universe! Put aside your gods as children put aside their puppets of kid and sawdust, when they discover that I, Mother Nature, can lay children of flesh and blood in their arms! Tear aside the veils of the "holies of holies!" They are just the cabinets of the wonder-working spiritualists!

*   *   *   *   *   *

In the difficult art of setting up a new god, Mahomet the
Arabian is undoubtedly *facile princeps,* for the difficulties he had to
contend with were appalling. So far as sacred things went, it was
in his land a period of utter indifference. Comic poets amused
themselves launching satirical verses, often of an obscene nature,
at the supernatural beings the in vogue. But in Homer's day the
poets were not above this sort of business, as witness the amours
of Mars and Venus as sung by Demodocus in the Odyssey,
deemed by so many critics as utterly unworthy of the great bard.

Had the sentimental founder of the Christian mythos
been in Mahomet's place, there would be no Christianity today.
However, in one respect they resembled each other, for they both
realized that setting up a new god was not a money-making
scheme. Someone must put his hand into his pocket to pay the
expenses of the exploitation of the idea. Many well-to-do women
ministered unto Jesus of their substance. Mahomet took a short
cut, he married a rich widow.

The next step was to impregnate himself with an odor of
sanctity — a very easy matter, if you know how. There are many
ways. Mahomet chose the easiest, retired to a cave for meditation
and the undergoing of ascetic hardships. It is claimed that he had
revolved the scheme of a new god over in his mind for fifteen
year. This is nothing. From the age of twelve to thirty, eighteen
years, the "man of sorrows" brooded over his idea.

Naturally the people of Arabia didn't take to the new religion. They were in many senses a learned people, good astronomers, good alchemists, good mathematicians. But Mahomet was a fighter, and he forced it down their throats at the point of the sword. After his victory, his solemn pilgrimage to Mecca was a masterstroke. Allah was seated on his shadowy throne, and today counts his followers by the millions. In forming his theocorp, too, Mahomet displayed the highest order of theotactic talent. In a land where it only rains every year or so, with vast stretches of parched sandy deserts, what could be more delightful than a promise that in the next world there should be fountains and green trees galore? Furthermore, in a land much given to concupiscence and lechery, what could be more of an entrancing outlook that a heaven peopled with a race of women that are celestially beautiful, forever young, wholesome, tender, and loving, with lustrous and deeply dark soft eyes, awaiting the arrival of the faithful?

One is most forcibly reminded of the reply of King Agrippa to the ex-Pharisee pleading before him. After telling him that his ravings were those of a mad man, the king, with a keen irony, cried out: You *Almost* (italics mine) persuaded me to be a Christian!

But after all, it remained for an American, one Joseph Smith, to set up one of the most original theocorps ever known to the civilized world, and it has had a really astonishing success when one takes into consideration that this vintage of Superstition was brewed, distilled, bottled, and sold at enormous prices to very intelligent people right here within the very limits of our Republic. Without any exaggeration it has made "the wilderness and the solitary place to be glad for them and the desert to rejoice and blossom as the rose."

Smith's heirs and assigns have literally "blue penciled" Jehovah, and under the guidance and control of a board of managers, consisting of old father Adam, Jesus, Mahomet, Smith, Brigham Young, and other "saints," with Adam as president, have set up a Celestian Manufacturing Company for the manufacture of souls, if possible at a rate commensurate with production on earth of bodies to receive them. These are no *homunculi* according to the recipe of Celsus, but the real thing, such, no doubt, as were in the days of old manufactured in the heavenly workshops of Jahveh himself. Later Jesus is to share his power with these "saints," and there is to be a temporal kingdom established somewhere here on earth. The very latest excursion of the human imagination into the bright fields of theotactics has resulted in the establishment of a very flourishing system of hagiopathy, commonly known as 'Christian science,' which is compacted one halfpenny worth of science and an intolerable deal of Superstition.

For centuries upon centuries there has been a system of healing based upon the really scientific fact that many of the ills which flesh of morbid nervous conditions, and are readily, at times, almost miraculously, cured by "shock," "suggestion," or prayer accompanied by implicit faith in the so-called healer.

Naturally the founder of founders of this faith had no use for the Old Testament, for the Jews, under the rule of Jahveh, were very fond of a good purge or a dose of bitter herbs. So far as Jahveh was concerned, these scientists simply reduced him to a mere abstraction. The most filmy and cobwebby summer cloud, wrung out and hung up to dry in the sun, would be more existent than the god of these new Christians, and yet with the courage of ignorance they say that god is love.

Now, love being a phase of consciousness (the only absolutely real thing, all else being mere postulate), or, better said, a state of sympathetic attraction between two consciousnesses, to apply to it the term "god," which can never be more than a mystic paraph, is willfully to substitute a theory for a condition — the infallible symptom of the presence of *bacillus sacerdotalis*.

Love we know and we can almost say *amo, ergo sum*. It is profitable to us even from a selfish standpoint; but god — outside of the lord's prayer — has never been known to give a crust to a beggar or a spoonful of milk to a kitten, not that many, very many spoonfuls of milk have not been given to kittens in god's name.

Poor, simple-minded, unsuspecting good men of the house of humanity, he never suspects the trick that is everlastingly being played upon him by the priest.

In the name of the prophet. Figs! But it is hardly fair for these "scientists" to attribute their miraculous cures to the school of healing as practiced by Jesus and his immediate followers and set forth in the so-called "New Testament," when thousands of years before that day healing by suggestion was practiced by the divine physician Aesculapius in the sanctum of his temple at Epidaurus. He actually cured the plague at Rome by "absent treatment," merely directing the embassy that entreated him to "take the case" to carry back with them a serpent, that being quite sufficient, just as Mrs. Eddy or one of her priestesses might dismiss a suffering suppliant with a copy of "Science and Health," with directions to "read it."

It is not at all to be supposed that Jesus gave himself up with any particular satisfaction to the practice of healing sick people; but it is one of the few ways in which a god can give, to the minds of the common people, who are always the first to interest themselves in a brand new divinity, assurance of his godhead. Haphazardly he must play the physician, and that, too, without hire, for the common people are always frugal in paying for mere advice. But these cures soon become a valuable asset in the possession of any god or half-god who is determined to leave a record behind him, and Jesus made the most of it. When the doubters from the opposition camp began to quiz him, he simply said to them: You go and tell john what you have seen and heard, how the blind see, the lame walk, the lepers cleansed, the deaf hear, and the dead are raised. Poor wretched children of humanity, is this the best the gods can do for you? Hundreds of years before this the older gods had given you a much nobler and more positive assurance of their divinity, Apollo with his music, Ceres with her agriculture, Bacchus with his wine, Minerva with her wisdom, Juno with conjugal felicity, mercury with his commerce, Venus with her love, and the Muses with their arts.

Are you, children of humanity, to be forever tricked, first by one god, and then by another, with their hordes of priests living upon you, ready with a blessing if you will pay for it, or with a curse if you turn away from their altars in contempt? I cannot think it! The day must be near at hand when you shall ring in your wrath and drive out Superstition from your temples as you have driven out tyranny and despotism and human slavery from your fair land, whose blue arch spangled with stars of Liberty was never intended by your fathers to cover any other than a free and enlightened people, in whose minds and hearts degrading ignorance or baleful Superstition should never find a lodgment.

*   *   *   *   *   *

In all god-systems, from the very earliest stages of their evolution, there is a strongly marked tendency to construct a theocorp, so as to make the system practicable, for surely it would be a most undignified proceeding for a god to run about executing his own orders, doing his own errands, lighting up the sun, unloosening the winds, forging his own thunderbolts or conducting souls to their last abiding-place. In the Egyptian and Babylonian theocorps, winged creatures, at times of the most fantastic forms, are met with, and the Jews, who always took good care to profit by their enslavement among superior peoples, brought away their first notions of winged creatures from the Babylonian captivity. These greatly enriched their celestial furnishings, and Jahveh proceeded to make good use of them, and there is no better proof that Moses did not write Genesis than upon driving Adam and Eve out of Eden. Jahveh, long before he acquired them is made to place "cherubim" at the cast of the garden and arrange a flaming sword, apparently a revolving one. All this is seemingly an exaggerated precaution to take against poor Adam; but it must be borne in the mind that he was between thirty five and forty feet in height.

But the "seraphim," another form of winged creature, were hexapterous. With one pair he — for there were never any creatures of the female sex allowed in the Jewish theocorp — covered his face, with the second pair he covered his feet, and with the third he performed aviation.

Later the Jewish theocorp was enriched with a simpler form of winged beings denominated in the Septuagint *aggeloi (Dios aggeloi)*, and the Greek translators appropriated the term, just as they took hundreds of others which afterwards became famous, e.g., ecclesiastic, baptize, Christ, episcopal, dogma, Eucharist, presbyter, etc. Unlike many of the winged creatures of the Olympian theocorp, such as the rosy boy-god Eros with his baby wings, the exquisite Psyche with her filmy fans, the dainty Iris with her rainbow-tinted pinions, and the "lackey of the gods," with petasus and talaria, poised on a "heaven-kissing hill," the *aggeloi* of the Jewish mythology were male beings of great strength and stature, as evidenced in the catch-as-catch-can between Jacob and an angel, who, after a long struggle, threw Jacob's thigh out of joint. John the seer witnessed thousands and thousands of angels round about the throne and heard their voices. There were angels of destruction, ready at a sign from Jahveh to wipe a city or a people from the face of the earth. Like Father Jove's lesser gods these angels had luminous faces, and often appeared to mortals, and in visions were seen descending from, and ascending to, heaven, But now that the children of Superstition are obliged to find a higher location than the banks of mist a mile or so above the earth's surface, it would naturally be ridiculous to expect angels to come as often as formerly, their visits being now "short and far between," and likely to cease altogether as education and enlightenment destroy the poisonous miasmata that have drifted over our land from the Mediterranean stew-pan of ignorance and Superstition

As has been the case in all celestial regions, inhabited by whole gods, half gods, angels winged and not winged, and monsters compacted of half human, half beast, or whole beast such as John the seer describes, having seven heads and ten horns, with a tail strong enough to knock one-third of the stars out of their settings and tumble them down to earth, rebellions break out. John was "war in heaven," a chief of angels named Michael leading his angelic cohorts against Satan and his angels, Satan being worsted and cast out into the earth.

And a writer named Jude tells of a conflict between Jahveh and certain angels and how he loaded them with everlasting chains, and how this same archangel Michael had dispute with Satan in relation to the "body of Moses."

Prometheus, in his contest with father Jove, tells how a feud was stirred up among the divinities. How Father Jove was in his wrath bent upon destroying the whole race of mortals. As the great Greek dramatist puts it: Everyone that has new-acquired power is stern.

When the Christians sought to destroy the gods of Greece by taking over the Jewish mythology *en bloc,* they proceeded to make some very considerable changes in the component parts of the theocorp. The cherubim and seraphim did not appeal to them. A being with three pairs of wings was not very lovely to look upon. It appeared too much as a gigantic insect.

The first radical change in the theocorp was to do something that very naturally would prove to be positively abhorrent to the Jewish monotheistic idea, that is to say, not only admitting the son and a mysterious being visible only to human eyes in the shape of a white dove into the theocorp, but introducing a woman (the mother) as Queen of Heaven, and filling the sacred precincts with swarms of female angels. Of course, as intimated by Jesus, there was not as in Olympian mythology any cohabitation between the male and female angels. No one seems to know how they increased or where the great numbers of baby angels came from, who constitute in the skillful manipulation of the priests, evangelists, and preachers of all denominations one of the great and irresistible means to an end in turning the minds of the young out into the poisonous pastures of Superstition. Shame! Burning shame! Will it, can it, must it go on forever?

*   *   *   *   *   *

The growth of the human soul was slow. The first gods that man set up were only satisfied when their altars were wet with human blood, the warmer the more efficacious. To please the god of the Aztecs the victim was laid close to the altar so that his heart could be placed, still palpitating, upon it. Siva, the third person of the Hindu trinity, exacted human sacrifices by crushing under wheels of juggernaut. Both Father Jove and Jahveh were not averse to human sacrifices. Both mythologies show that Jews and Greeks had well defined notions of its efficacy. At the last moment Diana relented and saved the life of Iphigenia when the knife was at her fair throat. Jahveh, too, relented as Abraham had already piled the wood of the burnt offering upon his son; but the glib manner in which he directed Abraham to take his only son, whom he loved, and offer him for a burnt offering, speaks for itself. But in the case of Jephthah, Jahveh stood firm, just as a god should do, and let his nostrils inhale the odor of this virgin's blood. In fact Jahveh seemed to take pleasure in these bloody deeds, for he raised no hand to stay the hewing to pieces of Agag before his very face, not to save Uriah when he fell in forefront of the hottest battle. The ancient Druid priests also delighted their gods with human sacrifices — a trick no doubt learned in the Orient. These "sacrifices" were the parents of prayer which they dipped in blood and which odor clings to it to this day, and no human being sends up a prayer in our time to these "shadowy gods on shadowy thrones," that he does not stir the foul, red mess of the olden time, and the thurifer wags his thurible to smother the sickening odor. Later the roasting of the slain beast took place of the human sacrifice, and the fattest tidbits were set aside for Father Jove and Jahveh, and the Grecian and Roman augurs poked their tongues into their cheeks as they pretended to inspect the entrails, while Jahveh's priests stood by to see whether he would deign to accept the offering by lazily kicking a bolt from his arsenal to signify his pleasure.

Now, now, there are no more left-over dainty bits for the priest; but the latter feels that his very existence lies in the degree of fervor that he can excite in the hearts of the prostrate worshippers. And so the old world wags on, the poor wretch of a Hindu sweating at the wheel of his praying machine, the Muslim prostrating himself at the call of the muezzin, the mumbling and anxious Romanist shifting the wooden balls of his rosary with trembling fingers, and the calm and placid Protestant half kneeling and with but partially covered face telling his god what a "miserable sinner" he is — which he doesn't believe himself, and begging him to save *his* soul whatever he may do with the *others*. Prayer is the offspring of sacrifice to the gods, and human selfishness is its mother, and in its place it generated Superstition with ignorance for the mother.

Let mam nut think for a moment what vile and despicable uses he would put his god to, were he able to sway him by prayer — *particeps* in murder and assassination; ally in iniquitous war, oppression and pillage; cover in unthinkably villainous deceit, treachery and chicanery; colleague and zealous stand by in the slaughter and fury of every holy war. For us to apply for assistance to a power, which is so obviously of our own creation and which we have under the subtle guidance and minatory prompting of the priests dubbed "superhuman," and at the command of these latter day silversmiths must stand ready at a sign at any moment to shout: Great is Diana of Ephesians! Is so illogical, so ridiculous, so plainly a part of mere scheme to preserve intact certain fees, perquisites and emoluments, that one wonders how self-respecting and ration human beings can still be held down to these appeals to a deity.

Of course, we may expect anything from the human mind when it has been for centuries soaked, steeped, and sodden in the stew-pan of Superstition and debauched by promises of a certain and sure entry after death into a *pays de Cocagne.*

But in the name of enlightenment humanity — as free from the oppressor's shackles as we are from the binding effect of hoary precedent — let us spread it upon the record that we do not belong to such a class of human beings.

We have gone far enough as it is. What has been the result of these "prayers," these appeals to this "superhuman power" for help? What could it be but a steady trickle of hypocrisy, soaking into very tissue of our bodies politic, social and ethical? We are tossed by one horn or the other of the dilemma — when these omnipotent beings do not help us after our prostrations and supplications, we are forced to do one thing or the other, despise them, flout them, and chastise them, as does the African savage, logical in his underdeveloped intelligence, or apologize for them. To the debauchment of our own intellects, to the glaring defilement of our own human dignity, to the merciless blotting out of our own human self-respect, we do apologize for them. Were this god a man and he so failed us, we would hold our knuckles beneath his nose and call him a "lying fraud" and a "cheat" and an "impostor."

But what must we do now at the bidding of the priest in order to save the credit of this "omnipotent being" who has tricked us, led us on, and then abandoned us to the contumely of a world, only too ready to gloat over the misfortunes of a fellow creature? Either we must take the entire blame upon ourselves — no matter how sacred our cause is to us — or cry out that he is punishing us for our sins or the sins of our fathers, and we did not deserve his help!

Or, we must save his credit by bowing our heads at the sign of the priest and murmur humbly and contritely: His ways are past finding out; the wisdom of this world is foolishness with god; though he slay me yet will I trust him: whom he loves, he chastened; the battle is not to the strong; it is not in man to direct his steps; all nations before him are as nothing; you render to every man according to his work.

There could not be a better illustration of the utter futility of that "effeminate uplifting of hands," as the Greek dramatist terms it, than in our Civil War. The sentimental side was the South's, they were fighting for their liberty, and we had ten to their one. If ever that touching expression of Virgil's, *lachrime rerum*, found a fitting application it was here. The fair women of the Southland deluged Jahveh's altars with their bitterest tears, and their deep-drawn sighs gathered like a mist upon the stained-glass windows of his temples, shutting out the sunshine and rolling down in drops of supplication, gracious enough to move a Moloch. They might as well have addressed them to the mid idol of an African savage. Poor sweet souls, they didn't know and probably don't know now that gods follow and never lead; and that they can't help liberty when the tyrant has the cannon of the longest range.

My countrymen, why not be honest? If you could but once free your souls from the grievous burden of these Superstitions, you would stand up refreshed and strengthened like men who have shed the light of some bad disorder and again walk forth in the health and sweetness of purged bodies and clear skins.

Would not it be a thousand times better to address your prayers to those who can hear them and be moved by them, to those we love, to those whom we honor and respect, to those who can lift us up and strengthen us with their thoughts and influences, to those who can turn us away from the hurtful and towards the healthy, to those who will prompt us to good actions and lead us to live for someone else than yourself?

The "Lord's Prayer" is obviously artificial and manifestly put together by an illogical and unthinking mind, bent upon glorifying a god and not, as it should be, upon the betterment of mankind. Man should eat the bread of toil. It should not be a god given. To attach a condition to human forgiveness places it on a lower scale than the dog's, who puts all his thoughts on the future and has none for the past.

"Lead us not into temptation" might be addressed to a demon that haunts our pillow or our path, but not to an omnipotent god. And the prayer should have ended: "And of thy power and of thy kingdom, make us the glory."

*   *   *   *   *   *

The more ignorant and degraded the human mind is, the more it cries after the miraculous, and from the setting up of the first rude altar, unhewn and shapeless, the gods have been unceasingly occupied, under the direction of the priests, either in comforting or destroying their worshippers, destroying them by fire, flood, pestilence, famine, and the play of thunderbolts; or comforting them by an almost perpetual show of petty miracles in the daily walks of life. Man paid for them, and the priests were forced to keep up the supply. All religions being "made on earth," you may imagine how silly and ridiculous most of these miracles were, especially in the Jewish mythology. In fact, in wonder-working, Jahveh was rarely so grand and picturesque as Father Jove, that is, with very few exceptions, the one being Joshua's ordering the sun to stand still while he continued the slaughter of the enemy; but this miracle has no beauty in the eyes of an intelligent man, I had almost said "or child," who knows that were the earth to be arrested in its revolution for the thousand-millionth of a second, it would tumble into the sun.

Dividing the waters of the Red Sea and making a dry path for the Jews to cross over to the opposite shore would have been rather a taking miracle had it not been followed by one of the vilest and shabbiest tricks, viz.: allowing the Egyptians to get halfway across and then turning the waters back upon them. A god should always bear in mind that he is expected to be above human weakness and human passions.

In this respect Jahveh fails far below Father Jove. As he says himself he is a "jealous god," and he might have added, cruel, revengeful, and bloody-minded; in fact, a tribal god in every sense of the word, ever ready to play some trick or stratagem upon the enemies of the twelve tribes under his special guidance, and quite satisfied to hang in the form of a cloud over the tent containing such mystic paraphernalia as nomadic tribes could conjure up. Let us fondly hope that the day is not far distant when some master mind will, by the lightning of his intellect, dissolve all "clouds" of Superstition that hang over our civilization just as the Roman general entered the so-called "holy of holies" and lifted the veil to show the world that there was nothing behind it. Jahveh had not even one last thunderbolt left to hurl at him, although he had, once upon a time, for a mere touch of ark by a profane hand, stricken the man dead.

And such someday must be the fate of all "holies of holies," set up by the priests to hold the human mind in servitude. The Jewish mythology often surpasses the Grecian and Roman in excesses pf cruelty that might well stagger our red Indians. Such as the she bears destroying forty-two children for a bit of mere mischief; sending down fire upon his people for a trivial complaint; slaughtering fifty thousand threescore and ten people for looking into the ark; sending one of his terrible angels in the night to slay a hundred fourscore and five thousand Assyrians, so that when they arose early morning, behold, they were all dead corpses.

The three men delivered from the fiery furnace, Daniel saved in the den of lions, Jonah kept safely three days and three nights in the belly of a great fish, and Balaam's ass conversing in excellent Hebrew with his master, these are but a few of the many Munchausen tales that made the Jewish mythology the butt of ridicule in the days of Grecian and Roman supremacy in literature, art, and refinement. And think, too, that a low-statured, misshapen, unlettered Jew, in the very shadow of the immortal masterpieces of Greek art, himself fresh from a fabricated interview with the spirit of the crucified Jesus, himself ready at a moment's notice to invent tales of miraculous experiences, should have had the audacity to charge these great founders of the world's present architecture, sculpture, philosophy, and literary models in every genre with being "superstitious!"

Superstition? Their Superstition was a sweet and lovely wisdom compared with the semi-barbarous attempts of a nomadic people to set the aureola of kingly majesty about the head of their god.

To compare the beauty, fragrance, poesy, exquisite pathos, wonderful wealth of imagery, delicious examples of devotion to death, music of nomenclature, indescribable coloring of surroundings, inexhaustible mine of physical grace, mental diversity, and soulful exhortation — light, airy, feathery, filmy, and gossamer fancies of mortal weaving, as well as the solid, deep substratum of equity, wisdom, and justice of the Greek mythology, with the Jewish, would be like naming in the same breath the sweet, fragrant, delicious herbs of the garden and the silkweed of the moor. And yet, this magnificent world of ours, in a moment of despair, having shed its ancient gods and standing naked of supernatural protection (to its imagined shame), put off its majestic toga that had held the barbarous world in awe and donned a Jewish gabardine, grimy with the grease and gurry of a thousand years of Superstition! Wonder not, enlightened sons of freedom, at this strange and shameful act that man, fretted and pheesed by bonze, rabbi, fakir, muezzin, priest, parson, presbyter, and medicine man, do not cry out as he should: Oh! A plague on all your gods! But yields him up to the new scheme of purgation and salvation without a murmur. Then again, politics throws him from his orbit, and he in his utter weariness lays hold of the skirts of the first poltroon who has a vision for the sake of votes.

Christianity, the moment it loaded itself with the degrading Superstitions of the Jewish mythology, became a grievous load for man to carry. There was no form of despotism, no flagrant violation of the rights of man, no outrageous suppression of the bounding force of the human intellect, no merciless slaughter of those who dared to contradict the foul Superstitions of this mythology, no decrees of death at the stake or by *peine forte et dure,* that could not be fully justified by the rulings of Jahveh or his successor Jehovah.

It poisoned the Common Law and made women the virtual slave of their husbands, who might coin their labor into shillings for their husband's selfish enjoyment, leave the marks of a lash upon their back, provided they were not seriously injured; thrust their head into the witches' bridle or blind them with a ducking stool. They brought these villainous samples of Jewish law into our fair and free land, and it is less than fifty years ago that women were so far freed from the domination of their husbands as to be able to execute a contract, or upon having been beaten by them to have them arrested for assault; and it is to the teachings of that misshapen little Jewish energumen Saul, that women are today regarded as moral and intellectual weaklings, unfit to govern themselves, prone to evil doing, not entitled to the custody of the very children that they bear, accorded as criminal by not a jury of their peers, but by their oppressors. And when peradventure, with Jehovah's nod of approval, linked to a man who proves to be a brute, she finds herself, under priestly decree, within the limits of the Empire State and of many others,

denied those sacred rights accorded the citizens of our Republic
— "liberty and the pursuit of happiness," and obliged in order to
free herself from her worse than actual chains to resort to fraud,
deceit, and perjury to actual circumvent the statute enacted at
priestly bidding. The man may steep his very soul in lust and
lasciviousness, and yet, when fresh-shirted, clean shaven, clad in
correct habit, sit beside, mingle with, and while in dance touch
the hands and encircle the waists of the chastest and the purest;
but let a woman fall from the icy heights of chastity, and, like
Lucifer, she falls never to hope again.

And yet, these gods who, as the priests say, sit somewhere
amid the clouds of summer or ride the blasts of winter, in their
anxiety to punish wrong and uphold right, where are they? Where
they have always been, nowhere, save in the imaginations of
those who set them up either for selfish gain or selfish
exploitation.

*   *   *   *   *   *

I once heard a man by the name of Moody, whose head
was set down so close and hard upon his shoulders that his brain
ran riot in its passion for the supernatural, a second Saul of
tarsus, say that from one cover to the other of the divine
scriptures, as he called the Jewish mythology and its Christian
addendum, there runs a crimson rivulet of human blood: Yes,
beloved hearers, and from cover to cover, form unchaste Eve to
the Scarlet Woman described by the howling dervish of Patmos,

41

as you turn over these inspired pages, there comes to your sense of smell the sweet, stale, and pungent perfume of the harlot. To anyone who has ever walked the Cyprian highway, it is unmistakable, as it floats out upon the pure morning air, that odor of crushed and wilted roses mingled with the oil of myrrh, the fumes of wine and the heavy and heady perfumes of sandal, cinnamon and precious ointments. That this strain of tainted blood reached down to the very founder of Christianity, we have contemporary and undisputed evidence, for the Jews openly taunted him with it, saying: "We are not born of fornication." Neither the men nor women of this "sacred line" would stand the test of even the laxest moral code. Look at their own record:

Eve, unchaste, at least in thought; Sarah lending herself to the vile schemes of her lying and polygamistic husband; Rebecca compelling her younger son to deceive a blind old father, and steal the blessing from his elder brother; Leah and Rachel and the two concubines and their children, mothers of the twelve patriarchs; Tamar, daughter-in-law, not wife, of Judah, by whom she bore the "twins." Through this very line comes the house of David. Old Jacob, in blessing his twelve sons, singled out Judah over all his brethren. "The promised land bore his name," says Jamieson, "but above all the messiah sprung from it," and he might have added, "through Pharez." Without that illegitimate son, won by Tamar through her pretty trick of wrapping herself in her veil and covering her face, we should not have had those two charming personalities, David and Solomon, and those who came after. What became of Judah's signet ring and bracelets that he gave to Tamar deponent say not.

Five generations from Pharez we reach Salmon with his wife, the notorious harlot Rachab, mother of the much admired Boaz, who, like old Judah, was caught by the subtle and unchaste Ruth (in actions at least). No wonder, for she was a descendant in the direct line of drunken and incestuous Lot by his eldest daughter.

David, the man after Jahveh's own heart, had numerous wives, but the one after *his* own heart is adulteress Bathsheba, who, harlot that she was in nature, had caught David's lecherous eye by letting him see how very beautiful she was to look upon *in puris naturalibus*. Everyone knows the vile tale how he murdered her husband and how he "funeral baked meats did coldly furnish forth the marriages tables," and how she became the mother of Solomon, who holds the world's record as the most married and most "mistresses" of the humankind.

As to Rahab the harlot, it is agreed by most of the commentators that she was the "Rachab," one of the forebears of David, and the conclusion is inevitable that Jahveh must have "foreordained" that his ichor and this harlot's blood should run in one and the same channel some fine day. The stories of Dinah surrendering herself to Shechem, of Reuben's defilement of his father's bed and of the unspeakable conduct of Zimri and Cozbi and their revolting murder by Phinehas at the command of Jahveh so that he might appease his own wrath and stop the plague, are all too vile to be related here. The javelin stroke of Phinehas should be described as a master (and mistress) stroke.

As to the story of the Levite and his concubine, it seems to me so incredibly and damnably foul and fiendish that the wonder is that any tribe of savages would wish to spread it upon the record of their exploits, let alone the chosen people Jahveh, one of the four great gods famous in theotactics — the other three being Jehovah, his successor, father Jove, and Allah.

The one harlot dear to the Jewish heart is Esther, who was soaked for six months in the oil of myrrh and for six months in certain "sweet odors" to fit her for the bed of that lecherous and unjust monster Ahasuerus, who put away a chaste wife to make room for her. It is a very pretty story in the sequel; but the moral is not fragrant, nor is it even sweetened by blood of the seventy-five thousand foes slain by the Jews. But the fact of the matter is that under the rule of Jahveh the "woman that was very beautiful to look upon" seemed to possess a dynamic force of character very much akin to the courtesans of Athens, the demimondaines of Paris or the geishas of Japan. They pushed their offspring with a keen and remarkable energy, and these children of love were dear to their fathers. Look at David, fasting and lying all night upon the earth in prayer, refusing to rise or eat bread, while Uriah's wife's first child by him was sick.

When we come to the new regime under the transformed Jahveh we find the scarlet woman still evidence, the woman who was a "sinner" who bathed Jesus' feet with her fast-flowing tears, and of whom he said that "as she loved much," she was entitled to the greater forgiveness; the woman of Samaria and the woman to whom he said, "Neither do I condemn thee." Very poetic and dramatic; but morals should never be sacrificed for a denouement. Nature never forgives, why should a god of man's creation presume to do so? Nature is never sentimental, she strikes no attitudes, sends no messages to John. She says: Break my laws and I will punish you. Cease and I will heal you. Man could give no better proof of the truth that he himself is the power behind the celestial throne than by the fact that he at times destroys his god by laying too great a task upon him or by summoning him to do a thing sure to injure the credit of his priesthood. Father Jove's priests were very careful in this respect, they always made his oracles capable of a "yes" or "no" interpretation. It is the only safe way.

Jehovah, the softened and etherealized Jahveh, was no sooner seated upon his throne than the priests, while bidding him not to let loose fire or thunderbolts upon the earth, not to wipe out a great city through the agency of one or more of his angels of destruction, not to smite the scoffers with disease or pestilence, none of all the, but nevertheless committed the most woeful error of calling upon him to descend to earth himself, in any form he might choose to assume, and through the agency of a daughter of Eve to incarnate himself. Jahveh, not a great lover of women, never in his wildest manifestations of affection for his people ever dreamed of doing such a thing. Only Father Jove had dared to walk on earth for that purpose. It was an awful risk, and could the priests have foreseen how the miracle would live to rankle in minds "sick with the pale cast of thought," they never would have sanctioned it; never would have given it a moment's serious thought.

Had the new god only been better advised, he would have at least imitated Father Jove and made his descent upon earth, in a form so poetic, so mysterious, so alluring to chaste imaginations that the incarnation might have been rather suspected than asserted, might have been an "it is said," or an "it is claimed," or a "one might almost say." But no, he came from his throne-room in the clouds as a tall, handsome, so to speak, god-like figure, one of the most dazzling and imposing members of the theocorp, not bearded, true, but male, masculine, muscular, manly, he gradually clothed himself in visibility, and his raiment assumed the glow of phosphorescent light as twilight falls; he stood in the presence of a dark-eyed and full-tressed maiden espoused to a just man.

Had I continued, it were needful that my pen be dipped in ink of crimson hue that the glow of shame should redden the page, for here was an act that smote the white and velvety cheek of female chastity a stinging blow, which still echoes in the ears of the self-respecting womanhood. Here was a deed that spat upon the modesty of mankind and outraged human reason and laughed it to scorn — a deed that set the horns of cuckoldom upon a pure man's brow; and as Gabriel spread his wide-extending wings there came rippling down the sides of sky-piercing Olympus the ribald laughter of the assembled gods, for Great Pan was not dead yet. The blood of that day's victim still smoked in the grooves of the white marble floor about the altar of Father Jove, the holy Vestals were that moment crossing the forum and the people were kneeling and kissing their shadows as they passed, and the sweet boy Ganymede, with laughing eyes and rosy fingers, was washing the wine cups of the gods in water that spouted from the rock at the stroke of Pegasus' hoofs, and the Graces had begun to dance before the king of gods and men. The deed was done, and there, amid the dark foliage of the tree of Superstition grafted upon ignorance, hung the largest and fairest fruit it had ever borne, red and ripe to rottenness, and mankind reached up and plucked and ate till the qualms of satiety checked them, and, as they ate, they spat the seeds out upon the rich black soil beneath their feet.

*   *   *   *   *   *

If the Jewish mythology were but illumed with the rush light of common morality, it might, in spite of its filth and obscenity, enjoy to a greater degree the respect of human reason, but almost from cover to cover, with here and there an exception, it is fairly encrusted with theft, fraud, deceit, and chicanery, and Jahveh is himself the biggest sinner of them all. Could anymore cowardly and dishonest acts be conceived of than the manner in which he caused the walls of Jericho to tumble down flat, and then instructed his people to walk in and destroy man and woman, young and old, but to take good care to put all the silver and gold into the treasury of the house of the lord? Now it may be seen where the world learned the gentle art of indiscriminate slaughter and pillage in war times. And when the kings of the Amorites gathered against them, Jahveh said to Joshua, fear them not, and then proceeded to cast down great stones from heaven, and killed more of the enemy than the children of Israel slew with the sword.

Can a god cultivate bravery among his people by telling them not to fear outside nations, that he has so arranged things that one of his men shall chase a thousand? Can a god improve the morals of a people by permitting a woman to steal her father's image and then cover them with her skirts and add the crime of deceit and falsehood to theft? Can a god increase the honesty of his people by informing them that they may sell the flesh of an animal that has died upon their hands to the stranger, but not to their own people?

Can a god expect to correct the morals of his people by such a code as the one Jahveh engraved on a stone tablet furnished him by Moses? Where are there any commandments on that tablet against harlotry, keeping a concubine, criminal assault, seduction, polygamy, usury, human slavery, pillage and slaughter in war, even of women and children?

Can any god think it unnecessary to punish such a bestial and unspeakable crime such as that of Amnon's? Can any god imagine that the good morals of his people will be the better conserved by reading such obscene descriptions as contained in some of the chapters of Ezekiel? Can it be possible that an omniscient god would not be perfectly well aware of the evil effects destined in future centuries to flow from such a command as: Thou shalt not suffer a witch to live? To think that this majestic world already in possession of the superb system of Roman jurisprudence should, even under the guidance and direction of a strongly organized priesthood, have permitted a petty god set up in one of the mentally and physically dirtiest corners of the earth's surface, so to infect it with the rabies of Superstition as to slay one hundred thousand innocent human beings, men, women, and oftentimes, children, at such a command! The world will never know the exact numbers that were slain, often two to three thousand in a single community, under most appalling torture. Why didn't this "jealous" god, so anxious always to keep all of the other gods out of his domain, hurl one of his thunderbolts or even a huge stone, as he had done before, when assisting his people in battle, straight at the head of Witch of Endor, at that famous *séance,* and get, *himself,* the credit of having killed at least one witch? And to think that our fathers brought over to this fair land of freedom and the rights of man this hellish Superstition, and that nineteen innocent beings, men and women, met their death as its victims before our father's eyes were opened and they realized that their minds were under the spell of inherited delusions which for the nonce had transformed them into monsters of cruelty! But before the end came to this sudden and tempestuous storm of Superstition, freedom's air was polluted by the terrible spectacle of one execution by *peine forte et dure,* the life of a brother man crushed slowly out of his body by superposed weights! Oh, think of the unspeakable horror of it! Giles Cory was his name, and a shaft of blackest marble should mark his grave to be an eternal reminder to the citizens of our Republic of the abysmal depths to which religious Superstition is capable of sinking; and not until out beloved land has been purged of this awful crime cringing, mumbling worshipper of shadowy gods on shadowy thrones, should that black column be replaced by a snow-white one.

*   *   *   *   *   *

Rechristening Jahveh Jehovah has not helped the world any, save as a diluted poison is less harmful than full strength. True the bloody sacrifices have been dropped, Jahveh no longer enjoys the sweet odors of roasting meat laid upon his altars, nor does Jehovah keep up the war upon the gods of Egypt.

However, as I have shown, the theocorp was largely increased by the addition of three new members and by great swarms of female angels — a thing always abhorrent to Jahveh. These changes naturally called for an enlarged priesthood, for it must always be borne in mind that the two always balance each other — god ridden, priest-ridden — and the poor, ignorant wretch has more prayers to mumble and more tax to pay to keep his soul in a salvable condition. It was, in other words, the same old Superstition, only clad in prettier garments, with altars gaudy enough to satisfy the most *exigeant* with a glitter of candles and glory of stained glass, past anything the world hath ever witnessed in the matter of temples reared to please the shadowy gods on their shadowy thrones.

But in spite of it all, Lazarus continues to rot on Dives' marble doorsteps, and the dogs are at their old tricks. The window opens and the bones are scraped off the plates for them. Let all the members of the new theocorp watch out, for the modern Prometheus is unchained, and he "walks upon the wings of the wind." Someday he may get so high as to discover, as did the Great Pompey when he drew the veil aside, that there is nothing there, absolutely nothing. It would have been expecting too much to look for an abandonment of the old Superstitions by the founder of the new religion. What is in the blood must out. Not a drop of his but tingled with Superstition. Prophets are virtually compacted of Superstition. They must bless with uplifted hand, they must curse by book, bell, and candle. Jesus of Nazareth had two defects that must ever make a prophet dangerous, he was sentimental and superstitious; the first saved life long enough to make a career; the latter rendered him powerless to life man up a ten thousandth of an inch socially and ethically. Save my soul? Save my body first. John was brutally honest, and was cut short, as honest men always will be while Superstition reigns.

Look at the almost childish trick of the tribute money: Go to the sea, and cast a hook, and take up the fish that comes up, and when you have opened his mouth you shall find a piece of money, then take it and give to them for me and you.

Upon reading these words, humanity's lips are prone to twist into the rictus of a smile; but the smile dies and the groan escapes.

But there is even worse than this. Jesus gave full and absolute credence to that Munchausen tale of Jonah. He made it the very test of his godhood: An evil and adulterous generation seeks after a sign and there shall be no sign given to it, but the sign of the prophet Jonas, for as Jonas was three days and three nights in the whale's belly so shall the son of man be three days and three nights in the heart of the earth.

*　　　*　　　*　　　*　　　*　　　*

Our fathers dreamed a dream. It was to shut Superstition out of the Republic, or at least so to dilute its poison that in good time it might lose its hellish powers entirely. But it was too soon even to begin dreaming. However, much has happened since those days, and there is certainly a streak of light in the Orient of Truth and Enlightenment.

This Republic was never intended to have even the semblance of any religious bias. It was to be a purely secular government in the full sense of the term. Many of our fathers were deists, some agnostics and some out and out materialists.

Jefferson, in the Declaration of Independence, makes us appeal to "Nature and Nature's god," evidently meaning these words to be an implied protest against mixing up the rights of man with any form of revealed religion. The Framers did not allow the word "god" to appear in the Constitution. *Ex necessitate* it crept in on the margin in the A.D.

Early in the last century our Government put itself on record as being, strictly speaking, as much Mohammedan as Christian. In looking over the writings of Washington, I found but one mention by him of the name of Jesus. His theocorp, I imagine, was like himself an abstraction of frigid purity. It is said that he was once caught praying. If so, his powder supply must have been very low.

Instinctively an enlightened mind hates Superstition. He feels as a temperance man does among drunken roisterers.

There was an early movement in New England to kill the Superstition of the "virgin birth" by the propagation of Unitarianism and transcendentalism.

During my school days in Connecticut I have no recollection of ever having seen any church steeples or crosses; nor do I remember that there was any notice taken of Christmas or Easter. We boys had a counting-out rhyme, one line of which ran like this:

Harum-scarum, virgin-marum.

There being little or no priestly influence or surveillance, hundreds of Romanists coming to this country, especially Irishman, dropped their religion with their O's into the ocean on the way over.

Superstition sits lightly upon the shoulders of the enlightened man, and a single word will bring him to his senses. But now all is changed. Superstition, feeling itself in danger, has fallen back and thrown up the tranches of "privilege," "constitutional rights," "freedom of worship." Threats of anathema are hurled at the indifferent, and live curses flash about the head of the backslider. With that defiant air, so characteristics of Superstition, the priest now wears the scarlet badge of royalty or the purple of the noble, conferred by a triple-crowned monarch, allegiance to whom they do not abjure upon taking the oath of allegiance to the Republic. The more shame to them.

Nor are they the only Ephesians who are desperately shouting: Great is Diana! The Protestants, scenting the morning air of infidelity, as they term it, are greatly disturbed, although I fail to see how a man can be "unfaithful" to a god whose very existence he denies. They insist upon your having some kind of a god, although he be as faint as an idea of an idea. It isn't so much your soul that they want to save as it is the confession that you have one to save, if you should want to save it. They are like the drinking men who make a wry face when they see a man cold sober in their midst.

To sum up then, in spite of our common schools, academies, and colleges, in spite of our thousands of liberal publications, in spite of our libraries of scientific books, in spite of our lectures on the evolution of the universe, in spite of the spread of free thought and the manifest weakening of many of the old theories, yet Superstition still exhales a certain "odor of sanctity," and thousands of sensible men and women sit Sunday after Sunday and listen with grave faces to the reading of fabulous doings and monstrous tales that surpass the imaginative fertility of the Arabian Nights. Our children, fresh from their school books, from which they have learned that the earth-ball, like a gyroscope, is supported in space by the incalculable swiftness of its revolutions and that stopped for the thousand-millionth of a second it would fall, yet there stands the gowned priest drawing out the fantastic story of the petty Jew warrior; or the child, knowing from his physiology that putrid flesh is as dead as the rotten spot in his apple, must sit and listen to the tale of Lazarus; or, having learned to his delight from his Natural Philosophy how to create a rainbow, must give ear to that bit of priestly ingenuity by which the Jewish tribal god Jahveh is given the credit of having first for a specific reason set this bow in the beautiful summer clouds are but thin water mist tinged by the sunlight and floating over his head but a mile or so high, must he, to the wicked enslavement of his understanding, be forced to listen to the common Superstition of every tribe of savages, that here resides god surrounded by swarms of winged creatures, ready, upon the least justification, to hurl a thunderbolt upon the earth, when the poor child knows, too, form his physics, that lightning can only be generated at certain seasons and under certain conditions, and so on *ad infinitum et ad nauseam.*

But alas, this foul and degrading Superstition is legalized by the state, and priest and parson are protected in its dissemination.

Must it go on then forever?

I believe not, no, I'm sure not. There are unmistakable signs of a coming revulsion of awakened and outraged reason against these old Superstitions which have been for so many centuries kept alive and exploited by the agency of priesthoods for the acquirement of power and pay.

But we may hasten the coming of this to humanity, glorious event, the unshackling of the mind, the bestowal of complete liberty upon the intelligence of man.

True, we have no right to resort to the open assault of jibe and sneer, the "Court awards and the Law do give" protection to this Superstition, but we are not remediless. We may be wise and yet lawful conduct fight against this age-consecrated mental debauchment.

Let me enumerate some of the methods, and bear ever in mind that there is a terrible force in cold, calm, silent disapproval.

1st. Assume towards Superstition on any and all occasions, when not by your seeking you may be brought into its presence, the attitude of silent and dignified contempt. Enter no church or meeting-house where these Superstitions are recited or publicly proclaimed.

2nd. Attend no public meeting at least until after the invocation of any Jewish, Christian, or other god is completed, and take no part in any public ceremony where these shadowy beings on their shadowy thrones are called upon to "bless," as it is termed, the undertaking, which man has conceived and only man can carry to completion.

3rd. Show yourselves, men and women of free and enlightened minds, upon all occasions proud of your contempt for Superstitions of Jewish and Christian mythologies, and smile with deepest scorn at the cry of the latter-day silversmiths of Ephesus.

4th. Never outrage a friend's or neighbor's feelings by attacking his belief in these Superstitions. It is often a matter of inheritance, of temperament or inborn love of the monstrous and miraculous; but should you yourself be attacked, strike back with all your strength, dwell upon the long ages of mental servitude that the human mind has suffered under the lash of the priest; pour out your abhorrence of these filthy records of man's spiritual degradation and spare the miracle mongers not.

5th. Refuse to touch with hand or lips any book of so-called holy writ, or to lift your hand to the clouds or call upon the name of any god. The laws of our Republic will protect you in so doing.

6th. Ask and strive for the abolition of all oaths and appeals to gods to keep your testimony free from perjury and to punish you in the world to come if you swear falsely.

7th. Organize societies for the "suppression of Superstition," even though only two or three members agree to give some thought and labor in the good cause, particularly in organizing kindred societies offhand and orally, wherever a member may find himself or herself in company congenial to the work.

8th. Wherever an opportunity offers, advocate amendments to the fundamental law prohibiting presidents and governors from official recognition of any even or events in Jewish or Christian mythology, or the suspension of the sittings of any congress, legislature, court, or public body in deference to, or honor of, any such even, and forbidding the enactment of any statute for the punishment of so-called blasphemy, and the use of any public street or highway by any religious procession or parade in honor of any god, demigod, or person of any theocorp, or in excusing church property from taxation.

9th. Speak, write, and agitate in public and private against the outrageously unconstitutional action of our government in appointing so-called chaplains, or in receiving or holding any official intercourse with any individual, delegation, class, body corporate or otherwise representing any so-called religious faith and prohibiting any executive officer, national or state, from being present at, or in any way acknowledging the existence of any function having for its object the worship of any god, gods, or supernatural being excepting the particular system of theology to which he may individually belong.

*   *   *   *   *   *

The ancient and ever-ready objection to the abolition of a system of gods, no matter how crassly superstitious or highly productive of hypocrisy it may be, is the query: Well, what do you propose to put into its place? Man is, so they affirm, naturally religious, or, if you will, superstitious; take away his god or gods and he will run riot in crime and wrongdoing.

This is a terrible claim to make against humanity and as false as the existence of hell itself. All gods are alike, be they

Egyptian, Hindu, Babylonian, Jewish, Grecian, Christian, Muslim, or Mormon, mere masks for man to play his fantastic tricks of cruelty, duplicity, extortion, and oppression behind. Good men, just and true, need no gods. Make man respect himself and at one fell swoop you do away with the necessity of gods, heaven and hell, together with the thousand and one usual camp-followers — angels, archangels, two-winged or six-winged, devils, demons, goblins, or ghosts.

The fact, further, that many of the rarest, sweetest, fairest (in both senses), kindest, noblest human beings that have loved their kind and given their lives to succor, help, lift up, ennoble, and benefit the race have been unbelievers, gives the lie to this villainous slander.

But I accept the challenge, and in the next section I set forth a New Cult, of course in merest outline and most brief, as must be such a mere offhand sketch of a great scheme, and I approach the task, be assured, modestly and reverently, not with shoes off in kneeling posture and ash-covered head, but upright and confident as a man who walks forth after a storm, to lift up the prostrated trees in his neighbor's orchard, to plant new ones and to clear away the ruins and rubbish that the winds and rain have swept in upon his land; and above all, to tear up the roots, all bushes and vines that have been there so long as to lead him to imagine they were really a necessary part of the whole

*   *   *   *   *   *

LACONICS OF CULT

Be tolerant for your opponent's sake,
Be temperate for your body's sake,
Be obedient for your parent's sake,
Be studious for your mind's sake,
Be provident for your home's sake,
Be brave for your country's sake,
Be merciful for your animal's sake,
Be patient for your enemy's sake,
Be wise for your children's sake
Be loving for your wife's sake,
Be all these for your own sake.

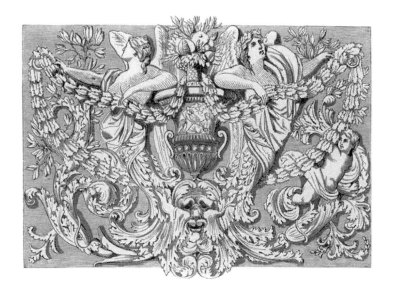

THE CULT OF THE IMMORTAL HUMAN

Take man out of the world and in a short time there would be nothing left but beasts and stubble; and all the gods that have for so many ages inhabited the insubstantial mansions of ever shifting and unstable clouds would ride out of existence on his last breath. The smile is inapt: there would be no such death struggle; they would pass out of existence like the soap-bubble of rainbow hue burst by the breeze of the mischievous boy's blowing. What would be left of them would not be more substantial than the fabric of the forgotten dream the morning after.

But not so with the world itself, for take man out of it and its most luscious and fairest cheeked fruits would revert to their poisonous and acrid originals; the lovely hundred-petaled rose would shrink to a button; the green and velvety meadow would forget its quiet beauty; the faithful dog, beautiful in eye and limb, would go back to the rocky kennel of wolf and jackal; the lithe-limbed horse, the soft-eyed heifer, the iris-necked pigeon, the thick-fleeced sheep would fade away to the rude types from which man lifted them. The noble grains would shrink to infinitesimal size, the succulent vegetables dwindle to fibrous knobs, the luscious berries part with their pulpy richness. Man, man who had found a desert and moor would leave it clad in the beauty of an indescribable verdure, and as the song birds found themselves deprived of orchard, meadow, grain-field, park and pleasance, they would lose their gift of song in the struggle for life. To take man out of the world therefore would be to rob it of its true god, for it is the human that is immortal, it is mind, thought, consciousness, soul that persists, rising ever higher and higher. Gods go down to their twilight and night, their temples fall to ruin, their altars crumble, their sacred writings on tablets of hardened clay lie in neglected heaps, but man the immortal human knows no death. Turned from one path he treads another; pyramids are but mile-stones in his course. Ever rising in power and dignity the human mind bursts from the chrysalis of one age to spread its wings in another. It is he that is immortal, for it is he that is the most supreme manifestation of nature's eternal development of lower forms into higher. For ages upon ages, he himself has been time, the gods are mere sun-dials; he himself the glorious dawn, all the "gospels" but the mere crow of the chanticleer; but the lying dial can no longer keep up the deception that it measures off its own material, nor the silly cock persuade the world that the dawn comes at its call.

*　　　*　　　*　　　*　　　*　　　*

This "sure and firm-set earth" is but a trembling quagmire and unstable sand compared to human consciousness. The earth may be there or not, we have but the proof of our senses; but our consciousness is absolutely real, it's the only proof of our existence, and it is so immeasurably above all the other forces of nature that when compared to it it may be said of them as Hamlet said of this "majestical roof fretted with golden fire": it seems to be but a "pestilent congregation of vapors." Worlds may drop from their orbit and be vaporized by nearest sun; but my consciousness shall never forget the finding of a pin on a certain day.

It is needles here for me to dwell upon the fact that in all ages the great thinkers, philosophers, and investors apprehended — and that of course without the slightest help or prompting from anything like scientific investigation as known to and understood by us — that there was something immortal inherent in the nature of man. Their conclusions were but guesses, but man at times is absolutely caught up by the immortal human and lifted for an instant to a higher potentiality of thought.

But we are no longer dependent upon these "guesses," glorious as they were; we have now the absolute truth as obtained after long, patient, and actual study of nature herself. From her very first crude experiments in modes of motion, there has been a steady progression towards higher forms until the immortal human crowns the sublime edifice of nature's uplifting, and so wonderfully complex and highly evolved has become the human mind that it is no longer bound by the ordinary laws of nature, but rises in its eternal persistence to a self-existence, to an entity quite apart and freed from all the conditions of matter, self-recording, self-preserving, self-controlling, endowed with retrospect and prospect, memory, will, and consciousness. This is *la fine fleur* of nature's growing, and its perfume is love, pity, sympathy, kindness, and that even balance we call justice.

True, this "eternally persistent" is but a highly evolved force of nature, and it is wrapped for a time in the cerement of lightly solvable and disintegrating matter; but that brief space of time is but its "Wanderjahre," its apprenticeship during which it may, if it strives, takes on new beauty, new grace, new aspirations, in its ascent to a higher plane of existence.

All human love lies but in remembrance, and if this "soul" can carry *that* with it when its earthly envelope bursts and sets it free, *then all is well!*

As an eloquent English writer has put it: So long as we can be certain that our actions and thoughts in this life will help to determine our conditions and our relations to those we love, in the next, we can afford to smile at death.

The scientific fact of the sternal persistence of consciousness is the simple concept that lies at the base of the New Cult. It is as free from al Superstition as the pure air of the garden is from the miasmata of the swamp. It will not, cannot shock the most sensitive mind that bristles in anger and disgust at the agency of gods, angels, etc., and, while it is natural, it is highly poetic in that the soul is not turned loose in some immeasurable corner of space where the millions of millions of departed souls have congregated but like the subtle currents caught up by those *antennae* only to which they are attuned in perfect harmony, the immortal human will be attracted to those he loved on earth, by whom he is expected and whom he longs to be with, and this thought will buoy him through life and influence him powerfully so to live as not to mar, spot, or stain the immortal part of him.

*   *   *   *   *   *

The sentimental injunction to "love thy neighbor as thyself" has piled up more hypocrisy in this world than can be measured. Love is not the creature of an outside will, nor is it, like beauty, "its own excuse for being." It may capricious or illogical, but its foundations are firm-set if we but knew it.

Besides, it is a non-circulating medium, and poor coin wherewith to pay a debt to a neighbor. It may flatter the giver's vanity and he may think that he has parted with something; but it was only a sop to selfishness. The New Cult's bedrock principle:

HELP ONE ANOTHER

Sympathy for, and interest in, are the very parents of affection for a fellow being. It is a waste of time and money to preach a gospel to those who are already persuaded. This is the "very ecstasy" of selfishness, the apotheosis of self. Jesus laid down the principle that it is "lawful for anyone to do what he will with his own." This most vicious principle has put the world where it is today.

To this the New Cult says: No, a thousand times no! We cannot draw a breach without robbing some one of air; we cannot gnaw a crust without making someone go hungry. The submerged quarter, or third, will stay under until the world comes to its senses.

The New Cult abhors illness; no one must eat his morsel unless he earns it. No man must cover his back with another's cloak, but any man needing a cloak must have it upon executing a promise in writing that he will pay for it when he earns wage.

In the New Cult there will be no ravens to feed anyone. Help one another means: You help me and I will help you, and if you are too old or too infirm to help, we will help you anyway. Now that you will not be called upon to eat less to please a god, you may do so in order to have some to spare for a needy neighbor.

The priest exaggerates human sorrow as the quack does inflammation, so that he may seem to effect a greater cure.

The man who doesn't respect himself regards his soul as a burden to carry without receiving any wage for his labor. Feeding the soul on Superstition is like hiring a child to be good by gifts of sweets. The only excuse for thinking of oneself is to think how you may make yourself more useful to your fellow creatures. Helping one another begets interest, interest sympathy, and sympathy love.

*   *   *   *   *   *

The New Cult I call "Cult of the Immortal Human," and it is based upon the now scientifically proven fact that man is the crowning work of nature, gaining every year in power of intelligence and insight into his own nature and its demands, that the old fable of his having once been a god and now some sort of a "fallen angel" has worked incalculable harm to the species and should be extirpated, root and branch, and that all celestial regions, with gods and theocorps inhabiting them that have been supposed to exist in past ages and are now kept alive in certain modified forms by the priests, were and are the creations of his imagination, and that the present system of gods is the most harmful that the world has ever seen, in that man's reason and intelligence have in their unfolding outrun the power of the priests to keep up the deception, and the consequence is that in tens of thousands of cases man, for policy's sake or form a morbid disposition to suffer ancient wrongs inherited from his forebears rather than struggle for their abolition, continues to bow down before gods he does not believe in and listen to the recital of fables from ancient mythologies which in his heart he despises.

The New Cult has no gods, no heavens, no hells, no purgatories, no angels, no churches, no altars, no priests in black coats, no bible, no prayer-book, and no dogmas. It appeals to man's reason and not his Superstition, to his self-respect and not to his respect of shadowy gods on shadowy thrones. It says to him: *Be your own priest, and the immortal human within you your only god.*

The followers of the New Cult will take the name of "humanists," "cultists," or "psychists," and be organized into corporate bodies of companies under the title of "Cult of the Immortal Human: Circle of _____," with a prescribed number of guardians, one-half women, and one-half men.

One admonitor and one or more assistant admonitors will preside at all functions. The home or meeting place of each circle will be entitled:

HUMANITY HOUSE

Briefly stated the house will be divided as follows, upper and lower parts, the upper being entitled: Hall of Light, with the motto: Who enters here must leave self behind.

Humanity House will be: Dedicated to the elevation and ennoblement of the immortal human.

Hall of Light will be primarily reserved for the weekly services of admonition and for the more serious gatherings of the society; but the seats will be movable, so that it may at any time be used for social and intellectual entertainments by the companions of the circle.

The lower part of the house will be divided into peoples' parlor, circle store-room, baths, offices, etc.

Peoples' parlor will serve as a reading room, club room, and supper room.

Circle store-room, a place for storage of all clothing, furniture, dried grains, canned foods, etc., that may become the property of the circle by gift or otherwise, for sale to or free distribution among needy companions by the store-keeper under direction of guardians.

Personal cleanliness being one of the obligations of the Cult, the baths will be, under proper restrictions, for the use of companions without them in their homes.

A completely equipped humanity house will have under its direction a garden, coal and wool yard, laundry, bureau of health under charge of physician, kitchen, etc., etc. Needy companions must render services upon assistance. Every department must be self-supporting. No salaries, as such, will be paid to anyone.

The great and underlying principle of the Cult will be to reach the soul through its mortal envelope. It is worse than folly to attempt to lift up a human being morally and spiritually while he is ill fed, ill clad, ill housed, weakened by intemperance, wasted by disease, or discouraged and embittered by some real or imagined wrong suffered at the hands of his fellow man.

The first thing to do is to convince him that you are interested in his welfare. The purpose of the New Cult is to apply the energy and money for so many ages wasted in the adoration of the shadowy gods on their shadowy thrones to the mental, physical, and spiritual betterment of humanity.

Each circle stands by itself and gives its entire service to its own community. This is the only way to achieve any real and substantial success in any department of human endeavor.

The visionary scheme of Christianity to convert the whole world has hammered its love out so thin as to make it the jibe and sneer of every thinking man.

Some of the leading principles of the New Cult are:

1. Absolute equality of the sexes in every walk of life.
2. Minors above 14 to have equal voice with adults.
3. Plain life to be encouraged.
4. Physical cleanliness obligatory.
5. Vegetarianism advocated.
6. Public schools honored by a Laurel Day.
7. Patriotism: a lofty virtue in the Cult.
8. Children's chorus at weekly service. Special fests for children.
9. One great object: To bring the well-to-do and poor together so that they may learn to help one another.
10. Lifting up, purifying, and ennobling the immortal soul of humanity.
11. Lavations: or making clean the body to engender self-respect, for it is a principle of the New Cult that the first step to moral cleanliness is bodily cleanliness.
12. The word used by one member in addressing another is "companion," male or female. The New Cult regards us as "companions" on the same journey, some with fuller knapsacks that the others, but those with the leaner knapsacks having very possibly fuller hearts and stronger muscles. We are companions anyway.

MARKED DAYS IN THE CALENDAR OF THE NEW CULT

May 1st. Grand Memorial Fest and Spread (fruit, bread, and water) to celebrate the breaking away from the bonds of Superstition. Talk-fest after meal.

May 30th. Pilgrimage to the Graves.

June 15th. Laurel-day: Crowning of best scholars in the public schools.

July 4th. Solemn service in honor of liberty and the rights of man.

August 1st. Little Mother's Day in honor of the elder children who help to rear the family.

September 1st. Mother's and Father's Day. Fest and Spread prepared by the children.

Last week of the year: Fest of the snow-capped Evergreen (emblem of purity and faithfulness), fest of gifts and texts.

Last night of the year: Thank-fest for escape from hells, devils, and demons. Songs of choruses, etc.

Every Sunday: Service of admonition.

Every day: People's parlor

SPECIAL "MARKED DAYS"

Mid-year, June 30th. Prospect and retrospect.

Mid-summer, Soul's Day. Fest of the butterflies (for the children).

October 30th. Solemn contemplation of the higher life.

November 1st. Report day of humanity house in all its departments.

One side of the New Cult is interest in devotion to local government by the people and not by political managers. The teachings of the New Cult will be to the effects that local self-government is absolutely necessary to the pursuit of happiness by the human species.

The grand seal of the New Cult will be a triangle, on the left side of which shall stand the words: Humanity House, on the right: School House, at the base: Town Hall, that is: Man — Enlightenment — Local Government. The common emblem of the New Cult will be a butterfly with flat extended wings, as typical of the soul.

Such, briefly outlined, is the Cult of the Immortal Human. While pointing to a higher plane of existence, it never for a moment forgets the importance of the earthly apprenticeship. Beautiful deeds and beautiful thoughts can enhance the beauty of the immortal human. Interest in the individual's welfare on earth will touch his soul when all else fails; but it must be an intelligent, unaffected interest, not a mere sentimental sympathy. The New Cult says: I'm your companion in this journey through life; the mere fact that I am the richer doesn't change the relationship; the road is often steep and hard, let us help one another along. If I limp, let me lean on your shoulder; if your food gives out, fall back on mine. I'll help you in the cold, you help me in the heat. If I faint, hurry to the brook for cool water; if your shoes wear through, take my extra pair. It never was mine in reality, but I will call it so in order to get you to accept it.

Forward, companions! We're almost at the end anyway.

POEMS OF THE CULT OF THE IMMORTAL HUMAN

Note: These poems are given here for the purpose of showing how lightly and easily the poetic fancy is turned to the New Cult. I fell only too keenly that they are but a feeble glow to light the way towards an entirely new path. Maybe, other hands will add oil to the lamp and pick up the wick. However, of one thing be assured, they are honest of purpose and good of intent.

FATHER'S PARTING ADVICE TO HIS SON

In heart's best soil, this parting counsel sow,
And gauge my love in that I let you go:
Who has not bent the bow, knows not its force.
Go forth, my son, and test your own resource,
This life's a place where everyone should work
Lest some do double stent for those who shirk.
No one should empty a purse he has not filled
Nor use a shelter that he could not build.

End well the day that you have well begun,
Then only, may you count your task well done.
Weigh well your words and better still your deeds,
For words have wings but deeds drop fruitful seeds.
Deceive no man, even in a jest uncouth,
For jest may easy wear the garb of truth,
Be good to those who are good to you
Is often far richer than the gift that's sent.
Good actions with self-interest imbued
Deserve but simulated gratitude.
Be gentle, just, and firm. Avoid all strife,
Except to save your honor or your life.
Till danger bids you strike, withhold your blow,
Then knot your sinews and spare not your foe.
Be manly, open, brave, but lightly make
No quarrel yours for exhibition's sake;
Nor generosity display for looks,
Like scanty scholarship walled in by books.
Be tolerant and secretive in things
Wherein disclosure needless suffering brings.
Despise no man whose eyes with evil gleam
For men are often better than they seem.
Turn often your eyes and reverently scan
Where freedom graved the sacred rights of man,
And wear those lines around your heart entwined
So despot's rule stay hateful to your mind.
Though prizing woman's love, shun sudden flame
That often begins in bliss and ends in shame.
Sleep on your fancied wrongs, for sleep is a toll
To open the door of health and make you whole.
Weep if you will to moisten new resolve
But know it is sunshine that makes the earth revolve.

Eat as you earn with appetite unwooed
By spiced drink or highly-seasoned food.
Wine, though it surely be old man's crutch,
Is the young one's stilts; were better not to touch.
Love the night, best fitted it is for thought,
And waste it not in pleasure dearly bought.
Gaze on that faithful star that marks the north
When to serious things you go forth.
Loathe Superstition, boy, in all its shapes,
For every heaven has a hell that gapes
And every god sets scores of demons up
To tempt us with some passions-sweetened cup,
Or turn our thoughts from righteousness away
So that his priests may turn them back for pay.
In deep abhorrence hold the hand inclined
To lay a shackle upon the human mind.
Our country's soil's too pure, as you have read,
For sandaled monk or tonsured priest to tread.
Pay no heed to vision, sign, or dream
Foul scum of Superstition's deadly stream.
Offend no person's thoughts, but hold aloof
Where human knees are flexed beneath gilded roof.
Self's apotheosis! Whose clamorous prayer
Vibrates and dies upon the liquid air.
So fare you well! And in your pleasures' quest
Spoil not the immortal human in your breast.
Thus shall you bring me, in the higher life
The soul I gave, unstained by mortal strife.
Now, to your mother who does wait above
To set sweet seal upon this page of love!

SELF-ADMONITION; Or,
The Humanist's Reply to the Threats of Death

What's death to me, Child of the Immortal Light,
To whose bright, glorious day there comes no night?
The gathered strength of ages quickening me
Imparts the secret of eternity.
I need no help to tread the higher way,
I count the stars and measure world's decay,
The gods go down — that dim and shadowy race —
I set up others in their vacant place.
Not more than sunlight dreads the gathering cloud
Do I death's name, be it spoken ever so loud.
The tender flower that at his touch does die
First sheds its fragrant soul without a sigh.
Though flashing sickle slay with lightning speed
It cannot stay the dropping of the seed.
Of Superstition's brood, the dreaded chief,
His threats are empty and his stroke relief.
The Immortal Human, reason's source and stream
Does turn to vapor Superstition's dream

   *   *   *   *   *   *

Then let not sacred oil nor sacrament
To my peaceful couch in haste be sent,
Nor muttering priest, nor whining parson's prayer
To call winged creatures from the empty air,
Nor Superstition summoning her god
To mar my joyful shedding of the clod.
Not even an obolus for Charon's toll!

My other and immortal self, my soul,
Smile at death, him of the joyless mien,
And go your way, set free, sustained, serene.
My loved ones watched wherever I did roam,
Mine be the wanderer's joy at coming home.

THERE IS A KINGDOM WHOSE NAME IS LOVE

I

There is a Kingdom and its name is Love
In a land that's ever near,
And a soul dwells there of maiden fair
Whom I hold most passing dear.

II

That Kingdom is filled with a wonderful light,
Yet not from its palace or throne,
But only from glow of that beautiful soul
That dwells in that Kingdom alone.

III

For she is that Kingdom whose name is Love,
That Kingdom herself alone,
And some fair day with love for a crown
I'll come to that empty throne.

THE PRIEST'S FAREWELL TO HIS GODS

Fade, fade, you shadowy beings whom I crowned
As Kings of all, that I might consecrate
My right to earthly power. Go down in night!
For men at last have awakened to see the truth.
Fantastic children of the human brain,
Your reign is ended. Lo! I stand uncloaked
And stripped of power, your altar overturned,
Its last meat offering smoking in the dust
And like the Roman chief, Humanity
Has drawn your sacred curtains but to find
No sign or trace of you. Poor wretch am I,
Who have based ignorance to my profit coined.
Lo! Here I laugh you all to scorn! Where are
Your miracles, your wonders, signs, descents
To earth, your awesome words: Thus said the Lord,
The thunderous rattle of your chariot wheels
And angry flashings of your eyes, while the earth
Does, at your footstool rock beneath your ire?
I part reluctant with the winged horde
I act to guard your throne. The people loved
Them so, and when upon the despot's head
I poured the sacred ointment out, it was but
The price of a few poor pence to set a white
Dove free, thus sanctify the mailed fist
He laid upon the people. Ah! it was
So easy too, to stand behind the throne,
Your curses lightly balanced in my hand!
Ah! It was too grand and glorious to last!
And yet, content I cannot be! What's left
But curses of the plainest sort, no foray

Of thunder-bolt behind? Still, let me curse
Them one and all, even from Prometheus
Of old with fateful reed, and John of Mainz
With devil's pitch and Luther's dire revolt
Down to Columbia's hateful creed of mind's
Enfranchisement! Even gods must bow to fate.
You shadowy monarchs on your shadowy thrones,
It was sweet, that double tribute in your name —
I held both keys — to heaven's entrance door
And to purgation's exit. Now, behold
Me shorn, not like the Nazarite with strength
To grow again; but shorn forevermore!
Unless, ah, foolish dream, dense ignorance
And Superstition walk the earth again.
Then, then, dear gods, I'll call you back to life
And let my deepest cunning fashion forth
New creeds, new rites, new forms, new sacraments

CALIPSYCOPSIS; Or,
In Presence of a Beautiful Soul

Entranced, enthralled, I sit and gaze, beloved, upon
That soft and mellow light that does from out your eyes
Look forth, like morning's first timid ray or twilight's last
Mysterious glow! Speak not or you will fright it away.
It is music sleeping! O, touch not the string. The tone
Might be less beautiful. Stir not for fear it go.
Yet looks it out at me. It is deeper, softer even
And takes new beauty as I gaze. There is no word
To tell how tender how sweet it is! Shh! There,
It fluttered then and almost went out. Now glows again

So faintly. O, so faintly, yet it stays and takes
New color on, deep purple-like; and now methinks
I note in the air a fragrance, nameless as it is faint —
Like breath of maid who feeds upon the flowers she plucks.
No, close them not, beloved, still let me feel that light
That comes from love's wide-opened eyes that peered within
A darkened room in search of missing mate. It is
They ray that knows nor mete nor bound. You weep, beloved,
And through that mist, it faintly glows like morning light
Caught in the tear-drops of the night. It is gone! Not yet
It lingers in your smile. Sweet afterglow! Smile on,
Beloved, it lends a beauty to your face, so pure,
So sweet, you seem like marble sculpt, white, wintry rays
Adrift through rosy-tinted pane, illuming!
Was that your voice? O speak my name once more, once more,
A music new and strange lends sweetness to your tones,
Once more — my name, no, let me watch your lips, beloved!
Ah, now it is gone! The Immortal Human stirred within
You and the folded petals vexed the bud. Ah, say
Not so! You are still beautiful, beloved! How could
A soul like yours, though masked in dullest argil, walk
Unseen, unfelt, and unsuspected forth? The dull
And thoughtless throng, intent on self, might pass it by,
Even bide with it and feel its higher nature not.
But love would soon unkennel it, for mortal love
Can set its impress on the Immortal Human, lift
It up, wipe from its tenuous garb both spot and stain.
Cleanse it from earth's infection, strengthen, beautify,
Ennoble it, until in nature's own good time
Unfolding in progression infinite, eterne,
This life and its inheritance fades from the plates
Of memory as has existence precedent.

TO THE GRAND AND NOBLE SOUL OF MY BROTHER HENRY CLAY LOCKWOOD

You are not gone. Let filmed vision so
Proclaim, yet Love will not believe, for Love
Lynx eyed can see as deep as Faith; for Faith
Is Love although it bears another name.
You are not gone. Let dullard sense so will it,
Yet Love's keen ear does catch your voice, not stilled
To it; but mellowed in a minor key.
You are not gone. Despair's cold touch may seek
In vain, where Love's warm hand finds quickly out.
You are not gone. Like baffled hound, distrust
Turns from the chase; but with unerring scent,
Fed on herself, Love follows on the trail.
You are not gone. Doubt sips her own black brew,
Self-poisoned by the cunning of her art,
But Love, true love, lifts up Hope's magic cup
That never empties out while her sweet lips
Rest on its crystal brim. You are not gone.

SIT ASIMA TUA CUM MEA. SIT ANIMA MEA CUM TUA

You come like a beautiful thought
To the skillfully-fashioned mind,
Ah, could I but see how you are wrought
Even a glimmer of light to the blind.

Could your eyes gain a mellower glow,
Could your hands learn tenderer clasp

Than the gleam of the long, long ago,
Than the touch of that dear welcome grasp?

There's a chord that comes muted and faint
And tremblingly falls on my ear.
Ah! Would I could catch its sweet plaint —
You seem to be passing so near.

Ah, how can the word painter's arts
Senses of mortal man teach
The favor that sunlight imparts
To the Juice of the down-covered peach?

And how can a rose in full blow
Shut in a crystal clear bowl
Teach the beholder to know
The exquisite scent of its soul?

Sit Anima tua cum mea,
As close as the Immortal may bide,
Sit Anima mea cum tua
When I've passed over the Great Divide!

"TOO HONEST TO PRAY"

A radical friend of mine, in a moment of mental
depression being urged to embrace Christianity and give himself
over to prayer, replied: "Impossible — I am too honest to pray!"

(Written in my youth)
Too honest to kneel before altar or throne

And look for a harvest where nothing is sown;
Too honest to call himself vile and abject
When Nature says: "You are god — stand up erect!"
Too honest to close eyes, making day night,
Since error is darkness and truth alone light;
Too honest to ask for a heavenly cure
For ills that humanity loves to endure;
Too honest to ask for a crust or a cup,
While rain cometh down and grain cometh up:
Too honest to pray that eternal decrees
Be changed as a creature of moments may please;
Too honest to call for a balm from above,
While earth is all budding and blooming with love;
Too honest to dream of a life of pure bliss,
While workers and helpers are needed in this;
Too honest and brave in the battle of life
To falter while thousands are breasting the strife;
Too honest to think of an armor of prayer,
While bravest to think of bosoms go naked and bare;
Too honest to reach for a crown, even in thought,
While brows that are noblest of laurels have naught;
Too honest to rob mother earth of a tear,
While human hearts bend over the pall and bier;
Too honest to long for a realm of the blessed,
While hope is alive in humanity's breast;
Too honest to cry for a savior to save,
While brothers go down beneath the tide and wave;
Too honest to cringe beneath the lash of the priest,
Too human to tremble like fear-stricken beast!
Then give your brave answer whenever you can,
For more faith in god means less faith in man.

THOUGHTS. LOOKS. DEEDS

Note: The very Life and Light of the New Cult is: Help one another.

King thoughts are good, they lift your own soul up,
But pour no milk within the poor man's cup;
Kind looks are better, be of love no lack,
But put no coals within the beggar's sack;
Kind deeds are best of all, the soul's delight!
All the others may do well, but these do right.

O, EVERGREEN! DEAR EVERGREEN!

Air: "O, Tannenbaum" (Old German song)

For the children's use during the "Year End Fest" — Last week of December.

Note: It seems proper to continue the ancient Saxon custom of setting up a fir tree. The New Cult however makes no use of candles. The boughs of the tree are whitened to stimulate snow, tree and snow being emblems of Faithfulness and Purity.

I
O Evergreen, dear, faithful tree,
The birds return with joy to thee.
Your tents of green iin fields of white,
Await them in their earliest flight.

REFRAIN
O, Evergreen, dear Evergreen

More faithful boughs were never seen,
When wintry winds their harvest glean
You still are faithful Evergreen.

II

The rain may beat the towering oak
And strip it of its leafy cloak,
Or lay the mighty forest bare
And sweep its foliage through the air.

III

When wintry weather darkens sky
You sing the sweetest lullaby
And hold the snowdrift to your breast
As mother rocks her babe to rest.

IV

O, may my heart as constant be
As are your branches, faithful tree,
And may my soul be pure and white
As snow that decks your boughs tonight

ADMONITION
(Mother and child at bedtime)

CHILD
O guard me, mother, through the night
And lead, by day, my steps aright
That I may bring my soul to you
Unspotted in eternity.
Good night, good night.

MOTHER

Sleep, child of light, I'm ever near;
O, be not anxious, have no fear;
I'll guide your little feet aright
That you may set no stain or blight
From mortal pleasures strong allure
Upon your soul now sweet and pure.
Good night, good night.

Made in the USA
Middletown, DE
23 January 2024

48401371R00057